GUARDIAN ANGEL

ALL MY TOMORROWS
POETIC PASSIONS

by

LTC ROY E. PETERSON

authorHOUSE®

AuthorHouse™
1663 Liberty Drive
Bloomington, IN 47403
www.authorhouse.com
Phone: 1-800-839-8640

Published by AuthorHouse 5/30/2012

ISBN: 978-1-4772-1129-8 (sc)
ISBN: 978-1-4772-1128-1 (dj)
ISBN: 978-1-4772-1127-4 (e)

Library of Congress Control Number: 2012909381

Any people depicted in stock imagery provided by Thinkstock are models, and such images are being used for illustrative purposes only.
Certain stock imagery © Thinkstock.

This book is printed on acid-free paper.

Books Authored by LTC Roy E. Peterson

Albert: The Cat That Thought He Could Fly (Juvenile)
American Attache in the Moscow Maelstrom (Cold War History)
Between Darkness and Light (Poetry)
Fight of the Phoenix (Vietnam War History)
Guardian Angel: All My Tomorrows (Poetry)
Iron Ikon (Historical Fiction about US Foreign Commercial Officer Service/ Diplomat/Foreign Service)
Magnetism to Marriage (PreMarriage Relationships)
Russian Romance (Historical Fiction about IBM Penetration of Russian Far East)
Soviet Intelligence Process (Out of Print)

Books Planned by LTC Roy E. Peterson

American Agenda: Regeneration Blueprint (Politics)
Maturity: Mind Over Matter (Relationships)
Intelligence: Collection, Collation, and Communication (Government)
Order of the Delta Dragon (Historical Fiction)
Power of the Pentagon (History)
Precious Promises: Engagement Means Commitment (Relationships)
Victorville Visions: Development, Disappointment, and Drama (Historical Business Fiction)

DEDICATION

GUARDIAN ANGEL: All My Tomorrows

LTC Roy E. Peterson, April 2012

Guardian Angel is dedicated:

To all the angels I have known and some I never knew
A thousand pardons for the stress I must have put you through.

While the poetry enshrined in my first poetry collection, *Between Darkness and Light*, was slowly written and accumulated over half a century, the poetry contained in *Guardian Angel* is recent and vexed my mind over a year up to the date of publication.

Roy Peterson
Tucson, Arizona
April 2012

FOREWORD

If there were a fear factor, it seems to be a gene I never inherited. At the risk of maudlinity (I love to taste new words that seem recognizable, but have not been tried), I wish to give you a taste of why my Guardian Angels were kept busy.

At the age of two, my mother opened the door to the outside cellar in Belleview, Nebraska, now a suburb of Omaha. She went down to get some canned goods in Mason jars. I rode my tricycle to the entrance and then tried to ride down the steps. I made it down the first two and fell the next ten. On another day I tried it again and failed again. I never did have fear of trying it again, but mother never opened the door with me around. At the same age, one of my older playmates, one was Nancy and the other Diane, found discarded razor blades and my mother found me trying to use them on a piece of wood. Guardian Angels must have kept me safe.

Skipping ahead through several childhood mishaps, at the age of twelve I tried to ride my bicycle over the back of my aunt's 1949 Pontiac. For those of you who remember, the 1949 Pontiac Chief had a sloping back that I thought if I rode the bike as fast as I could, the wheel would go over the bumper and travel over the car. Needless to say after going full speed the bike stopped dead, but I did clear the top of the car and landed on the hood unharmed, just missing the hood ornament. My Guardian Angel must have been on duty again.

The same summer of 1955, I tried a new trick on my Grandfather's stable Monarch bike that had a flat carrier on the back. This time I was in town. The first time around the block I showed my mother, "Look, Mom, no hands." The second time around the block, I showed my mother, "Look, mom, no hands or feet." The third time around the block, I showed my mother, "Look, mom, no bike." I had tried to stand on the back rack behind the seat with my hands in the air like a daredevil, but crashed. Oh, my head was bloody, but I was angry the trick did not work and I had no bike to try it again. Thank you, Guardian Angel for the assist.

I belonged in the Vietnam War. I was shot at by sea, air, and land, but never felt fear, just anger at what the communists were doing to their own people. I often traveled the dangerous roads alone in the Jeep vehicle issued to me, but never even got a purple heart. I must have had a band of Guardian Angels watching and protecting. Some might call it bravery, some might call it stupidity. I just called it a feeling of invincibility.

I spent seven years in Russia on government service and finally as the IBM Regional Manager in Vladivostok, Russian Far East. In Vladivostok, known as the "wild east," there were mafia killings every week and bombs were set off. As the first US Department of Commerce Foreign Commercial Office in the Russian Far East, I had to travel to Moscow monthly to report and get funds. On the second trip there in September 1993, I stayed with the Director for Russia of the Commercial Service and slept overnight about the time of crowd activity and revolutionary activity to support Yeltsin as President of Russia. The next day I went to Kiev for a week helping to train East European local nationals from all the cities and regions. I flew back to Moscow to spend the night again with the Director. He and his wife walked me into the bedroom and showed me a bullet hole about one inch from where my head would have been on the pillow, or perhaps if I had rolled over that way, the shot would have been in the head. My Guardian Angel of the night must have messed up the timing of the shot from the street below by a twenty-four hour period and made sure I was gone. Thank you for watching me in Russia!

To say I have not felt fear is not the same as saying I have not felt a clear and present danger on occasion. I flew home from Fort Huachuca to Washington National Airport and was headed about 9 PM to my car in the middle of the parking lot. As I opened the door to my car, I sensed something wrong from behind. Spinning around I caught a mugger as he was attacking. I have not studied martial arts, but I literally kicked him in the chin and sent him reeling. I got into my car and reported at the gatehouse that I was attacked. No fear. Just anger!

In Russia I was on a back road about 20 kilometers north of Vladivostok and noticed a white Toyota tailing me. I sensed something wrong, so I took evasive action as I had been taught in my military attaché course. First I slowed down and the other car sped up. As it passed me, I slammed on the brakes and immediately flung the gears in reverse, made a spinning maneuver to travel the other direction and saw the other car stop, a person get out and try to hit my car with a rock. Missed! Thank you, Guardian Angels for my sixth sense.

The rest of the Guardian Angels are girls and women I have known, who all were special in their own way. The last one was my high school sweetheart still living in Texas, who found me in a hospital in California after suffering a poisonous bite that almost killed me. She was searching for me because something or someone was telling her to do so (so she said). We talked every day for three weeks and then she came out to California to get me out of the hospital and tend to me at home for two months. Thank you, Guardian Angels for telling Donna to find me.

Do I believe in Guardian Angels? Unabashedly and Unashamedly! The question is, DO YOU?

CONTENTS

PART V: RETROSPECT

PART VI: HOLIDAYS

PART VII: UNLOCKED TREASURES

PART I

GUARDIAN ANGEL

I BELIEVE IN ANGELS

by Roy E. Peterson (February 7, 2012)

I believe in Angels. In fact I've known a few.
I dedicate my words to them for everything they do.
I know I kept them busy just looking after me.
How many Angels do you ask? I think its
      twenty-three.

I AM YOUR GUARDIAN ANGEL

by Roy E. Peterson (January 2011)

I am your Guardian Angel now in everything you do.
I'll give you strength to carry on. I'm never far from you.
Just say a little prayer at work, or place that you may be.
Then I'll destroy the evil ones and make the demons flee.

I am your Guardian Angel sent down to help you cope
With those who want to bring you down and take away your
     hope.
Yes, I am on a mission here to keep you safe from harms
And save you for the one you love who waits with open arms.

I know you've felt my presence as I touched your inner soul.
The times when danger lingered near and I have kept you
     whole.
"Oh, Thank you Guardian Angel," was all the praise I need,
To touch me while I'm watching, and keep you safe indeed.

I am your Guardian Angel. I know you've felt my hand.
If there is danger lurking near, I call an angel band
To put their wings around you and keep you safe and warm.
I am a mighty warrior who can miracles perform.

Now please just pray to Jesus and He will talk to God.
He'll send a bolt of lightning and use his mighty rod.
The demons cannot hurt you or work when he is mad.
He'll use His heavenly powers to cast away the bad.

I came here to protect you. I am God's messenger.
I whisper softly to you, but I'm an avenger
To fight the hosts of Satan's hell, bent on deviltry
And cut the bonds of evil to set God's people free.

PART II

LOVE FOREVER

Photo Credit: Kristin Kelli Crawford
Kristeena and Anthony Engagement Photo

PRECIOUS PROMISES: NOW WE'RE ENGAGED

Dedicated to Kristeena and Anthony

by Roy E. Peterson (January 2011)

Now we're engaged and the world must know
We're a couple in spirit wherever we go.
A circle of two when we put on the ring
We gave to each other our everything.

The past is behind us and future ahead
We dream of each other when we go to bed.
We're focused together on things we must do
To prepare for our wedding and starting anew.

Engagement has strengthened our love and our will.
Now we're united our dreams to fulfill.
No matter what else, we already are one
In vision, in planning, in doing, in fun.

To our friends we say thank you for just being there.
Old flames are extinguished. We no longer care.
Our marriage is coming our wedding will be
Our final binding for eternity.

Photo Credit: Kourtney Kundrath
Wedding Kiss: Kristeena and Anthony Peterson

ALL MY TOMORROWS: WEDDING SONG

Dedicated to Kristeena Jo-ann and Anthony Edgar Peterson

by Roy E. Peterson (January 2011)

1

From this day forward, forever my love
I pledge to you darling and God above.
I'll never forsake you and always will be
Right here to protect you and keep you by me.

Chorus

All my tomorrows I give to you
All of my heartbeats, forever true
Each breath I take; each step of my life
You're walking there with me as man and wife.

2

Forsaking all others I give all my wealth
For richer or poorer, in sickness in health
I'll cling to you always as long as I live
With this ring I wed thee and all my love give.

Chorus

All my tomorrows I give to you
All of my heartbeats, forever true
Each breath I take; each step of my life
You're walking there with me as man and wife.

3

Though death will come dear and take one away
I'll watch you from heaven by night and by day.
Then we'll be together my darling once more
As we walk together on heaven's bright shore.

Chorus

All my tomorrows I give to you
All of my heartbeats, forever true
Each breath I take; each step of my life
You're walking there with me as man and wife.

LOVE IN THE AFTERGLOW

By Roy E. Peterson

Copyright © (March 2012)

As surely as the morning comes your future's looking bright,
But there will be those tougher times as surely comes the night.
The strength of love is certain. It weighs the pros and cons.
A temple made of diamonds that's stronger than the bronze.

When two hearts are in unison they know that deep within
The fire of love is burning though patience's wearing thin.
They work it out together and add another layer
Of armor on their marriage, as they embrace in prayer.

The fragrance from their union is something to behold
Far sweeter than the orchids, or even of the rose.
A fountain everlasting that flows from God above
Will always keep it blooming, for they have planted love.

PART III

LEGENDS AND LORE

Sammy Long
Official File Photo,
Texas Department of Public Safety

INTRODUCTION TO PART III

Part III requires an introduction to the legends and lore of a small section of West Texas that has survived through more than its share of knaves, nymphs, and ne'er-do-wells. From the gunfighters of the old west to the robber barons of the modern era, West Texas legends and lore provide a wealth of imagery.

I have chosen not to repeat the well known legends such as the fictional Pecos Bill, who fell out of a covered wagon and was raised by a pack of wolves, and who lasooed a tornado, or the real life Judge Roy Bean, "Law West of the Pecos." Rather I have focused on real characters from the town of present day McCamey to Pecos, a dusty, windy area south and west of Odessa, Texas. McCamey was the home to a 1930's oil boom that brought the giants of the industry to town and who would have stayed in town with their headquarters rather than migrating to the Odessa-Midland area, if the city fathers had not decided to tax them at a then unconscionable rate. From the 1920's and 1930's comes the tragic story of a rising circus performer and her husband who had a tragic accident. Pansy survived falling off the high wire with her husband who was killed, but she was never the same and stayed the rest of her life in McCamey. The legend of Sammy Long is that of the beloved Texas Trooper who was known personally by everyone from San Angelo to Fort Stockton as the trooper who cared for the teenagers.

The story of Maximilian's gold that was set upon first by Indians and then thieves as it wended its way across the Pecos at Horsehead Crossing just north of present day McCamey surprisingly has not received the national attention it deserved or the proper investigation into what happened.

Back to the mid 1950's and the story of Billy Sol Estes who bilked the government of hundreds of thousands of dollars with fake fertilizer tanks. I had the privilege of having as one of my debate partners at Hardin-Simmons University in Abilene, Texas, his small blonde niece, Nina Estes who took me to meet her father at his Abilene home and discuss "old" Billy Sol.

These four legends are taken from real life and represent the West Texas profile well. The last two poems are more fanciful: One about someone who was not there, but who had an ethereal presence and the other is a paean to Edgar Allan Poe, one of my respected "mentors".

THE LEGEND OF TEXAS TROOPER SAMMY LONG

A True Poetic Story

by Roy E. Peterson (February 2012)

Whenever West Texas tales are told,
Some speak of oil or Maximilian's gold,
Some of Judge Bean and his Pecos law,
And some of John Wesley Hardin's draw.

But I tell the legend of Sammy Long
A highway patrolman big and strong.
Who lived in McCamey, a West Texas town
And married the HomeEc teacher, Miss Brown.

The kids all thought they were getting away
With races by night and tricks by day.
For some reason it never occurred to us,
Sammy would talk to our parents and discuss—

What they should do and please don't tell
That Sammy knew our deeds and us very well.
The kids didn't know how the parents found out
What they were doing and what they were about.

Sammy protected the kids from shame,
But everyone knew who they should blame
For whatever happened and he would know
Who did what to whom at the drive-in show.

You better not speed or drive while drunk
Or you might end up in Sammy's trunk.
As kids we had a healthy fear
Of Sammy, but yet we felt secure.

A California stranger one fateful day
Was stopped by Sammy on the Rankin highway.
Sammy didn't know that he was on the run,
But the stranger opened fire with a .32 gun.

A shot hit Sammy and brought him down.
The stranger shot six times in his back on the ground.
A deer hunter saw what was going on
And that a stranger shot Sammy Long.

The man was returning from a hunting trip.
He took out his rifle and he fired a clip.
The report said the hunter shot the stranger dead
With lots of bullets. He was full of lead.

All in McCamey mourned the friend they had
With tears from every mom and kid and dad.
I like to think Sammy still rides erect
On the roads of West Texas to serve and protect.

Pansy (Fannie) Carpenter:
Circus Performer on the Trapeze
Circa 1926
Photo Credit: Janice Rice

THE TRAPEZE ARTIST WHO NEVER LEFT

DEDICATED TO THE MEMORY OF PANSY

(FANNIE CARPENTER)

By Roy E. Peterson (April 1, 2012)

The first time that I saw her I asked who could she be.
A shambling dirty woman you never hope to see.
Her hair was long and scraggly. Her dress was long and torn.
I wondered when I saw her, who could look so all forlorn.

She was pulling a dark red wagon, a Radio Flyer toy,
Along an unpaved alley, while staring at some boy.
I saw her then stoop over and pick up a tin can.
The boy got out of there quickly as far away he ran.

I followed at a distance; I had never seen such sight
In this West Texas setting, it just did not seem right.
She found a piece of junk there and figured it was good
And as she shuffled along, she checked the bins for food.

I learned they called her Pansy, but never found out why
Her name was changed from Fannie. I didn't want to pry.
Her house was old scrap lumber; a shack in an oil town,
Where both she and the town folk had better days there known.

The kids all called her crazy. The boys would tease and run.
The rumors were that Pansy could really shoot a gun.
My parents new to Texas in the '50's talked to her,
While I sat in the back seat of the car a listener.

My parents asked what they could do to help her in her need.
She said she needed nothing, but thank you for the deed.
Although her voice was gruff like, she had a softer side.
That changed my mind about her. I'm sure she had her pride.

She was a living legend, depends how old you are.
She arrived there in McCamey in a Ford A model car.
Her named was Fannie Carpenter and yes it was a fact.
Her husband made the duo for their high wire act.

The oil came in gushers and there was so much crude
10,000 quickly rushed there, the strong, the brave, the shrewd.
They needed entertainment, so a circus with its duo
Displayed the Flying Carpenters who put on quite a show.

Sweet Pansy was a beauty, long curls cascading down
Her golden tresses blowing as they drove first into town.
With shoulders bare through windows, she was like a movie
    star.
The men would look with longing as she travelled in the car.

In 1926 McCamey, they flew on their trapeze
And walked the tight rope lightly and did their act with ease.
But one night something happened to the two so well renowned.
Without a safety net they fell; their bodies hit the ground.

Her husband tried to save her and as they hit the earth,
He cradled her above him and kept her from sure death.
But Pansy hit her head hard, her head was injured bad.
Her husband died most instantly some think it drove her mad.

She never left McCamey as every day she'd grieve.
She felt her soul was stuck there, his grave she couldn't leave.
Though hundreds tried to court her, she never let them stay
Politely she would thank them and send them on their way.

She could have lived with family in Medina County where
She grew up, attended school, but she would not go there.
A recycler before the word came into the lexicon,
She built her own small house there with lumber she had sawn.

She was self sufficient, although she was petite.
She built on a garage there and set the Ford in concrete.
A monument to her husband, who had saved her life that night,
She never learned to drive it, but kept it out of sight.

She could not make a living back with the circus tent.
So she built little houses for oilfield workers rent.
They say that she put wood doors upon discarded cars
And rented them to desperate men who had to sleep in bars.

There was a dearth of housing in those early years out there
Where fire ants and rattlers were more than one could bear.
Pansy sewed the curtains and there are testaments
She added on the porches and turned tin to ornaments.

Her beauty sadly faded, her renters came and went
Just like the dream attraction had left the circus tent.
She became a scavenger for bottles and for tin,
For boards and metal roofing, and looked in every bin.

They say that every now and then when her funds were low
She'd walk the 94 miles to the town San Angelo,
Where she would do her banking and could be seen beside
The highway there a walking and never take a ride.

The few who went to see her said on her behalf
She looked like Mary Pickford in an aging photograph
That sat on a piano a memento of her past.
A reminder of her beauty and things that cannot last.

Though children were afraid there was no cause for alarm.
It was only her appearance. She never meant them harm.
She often shared with others the things that she would find
The one's she thought were worse off---The deaf, the dumb, the blind.

In failing health no longer could Pansy live alone.
She sold the Model A then, the only car she'd owned.
She left her life of sorrow and living second rate
And died in Kerrville hospital at the age of 78.

The town remembers Pansy, an eccentric character.
But I have seen the vision of the beauty that was her.
Within my heart are images I wish I could dispel
And hope she went to heaven, since living was her hell.

HOW MAXIMILIAN LOST HIS TREASURE

by Roy E. Peterson (April 2012)

The only Imperial Treasury lost in the American West
Purportedly was never found, but many have been obsessed.
The Civil War was raging and while restoring order,
The US with its trouble could not look beyond its border.

Meanwhile in France Napoleon the third had won election,
And abolished the Republic and with a single action,
Declared himself the Emperor of the Second Empire there,
But an Emperor without Empire was more than he could bear.

The nephew of Napoleon did something quite absurd
As France allied with Mexico, another Empire he declared.
While America was diverted and focused on its war,
Napoleon seized control there in 1864.

He selected for sub-Emperor the Archduke Ferdinand
To go there with Carlota and control the foreign land.
So Ferdinand Maximilian moved to Mexico
And called himself the Emperor with his inflated ego.

To be a Duke in Austria was really common fare,
But add the title, Emperor, and you had something rare.
He seized on opportunity that fell into his lap.
It's said that neither one could find the Empire on a map.

The move was but good politics with Max's brother Franz
The Emperor of Austria to help align with France.
The excuse for taking over was default on the debts
That Mexico owed foreign banks and had no more assets.

At first the wealthy landowners were ones supporting Max,
But liberal reforms of Juarez, he just would not rollback.
The Republicans of Juarez who had lost their government
Hated that an Austrian with French troops had been sent.

The Civil War had ended and by 1866,
Attention turned to Mexico and Latin Republics.
America told Napoleon, get French troops out of there
And take out Maximilian or else they best beware.

Now Max who was no dummy decided to retire
To his castle back in Austria and get out of the fire,
But to be a proper gentleman he needed to be rich.
A mountain of gold and silver he thought would do the trick.

It could not go to Veracruz. It would arouse suspicion.
He had to send it secretly with a military mission.
The cover used was bags of flour and barrels for disguise
And tell the wagon masters to hide from prying eyes.

The treasure passed Presidio on its way to Galveston,
Where ships were waiting patiently to take the treasure on.
The Rio Grande was passable at that time of year.
They headed into Texas, a Wild West frontier.

The fifteen wagon convoy was guarded by just four
Austrian soldiers riding. They should have sent some more.
Soon after reaching Texas somewhere across the Rio,
They met Confederate soldiers escaping to Mexico.

The men were from Missouri and told what lay between
The wagon train and San Antone and all that they had seen.
As they were riding southward they met some bandit gangs
And six reported Indians a riding on mustangs.

The Austrians hired the Missourians for protection of the "flour".
The Missourians got curious and wondered at their ardor.
No doubt it seemed quite strange to them that "flour" had an escort,
Especially of Austrians of the military sort.

One night near Horse Head Crossing along the Pecos bank
Five Missourians lured the guards away, the sixth came from the flank.
He moved between the wagons with his metal tools
He pried the barrels open and saw the gold and jewels.

When he reported what he'd seen to the conspirator
They decided that the Austrians they soon would overpower.
They made a pact to share the loot and then they made a plan
That they would strike the next day and take all that they can.

Six wagons they could manage with all the teamsters dead
And all the Austrians shot to death some miles from Horse Head.
The following night the caravan was camped at Castle Gap
A cut between the mesas. A place marked on their map.

Two Austrian were sleeping, while two were standing guard.
The fifteen Mexican teamsters were sleeping pretty hard.
Four shots rang out and killed the guards before they knew what hit.
And then the fifteen teamsters took the second hit.

Nineteen men were slaughtered. No one was left to fight
And then the band of soldiers decided there that night
They could not move the wagons and outride on the side.
A bad idea to kill the teamsters with fifteen tons to hide.

They moved the treasure nearby and released the oxen teams.
Then they hid the treasure, the stuff that's made of dreams.
It took a while to dig the pit and bury all the loot
An entire Imperial treasury and 19 dead men mute.

Each man had packed his horses with all the coin they'd carry
And headed out for San Antone for Indians being wary.
When two days they had ridden one of the men got ill
He dropped out for a rest. It's said they shot him on a hill.

There was no trust among them, they figured he'd return
To the buried loot and take it from the place the wagon's burned
To mark the treasure hidden beneath the sandy soil
In some forsaken canyon beneath the charred topsoil.

They continued on without him assuming he was dead,
But the wounded man recovered from the bullets made of lead.
He headed toward San Angelo, the first fort on the way
Along the trail to San Antone by night and not by day.

He struggled cross West Texas along the trail and then
He came upon the bodies of the five Missouri men.
Their saddle bags were empty and scattered all around
Perhaps Comanche raiders had left them on the ground.

He was the last survivor of a total twenty-five
Who had started on the journey and he was scarce alive.
He kept on struggling forward and one evening saw a fire
A camp set up by horse thieves; his circumstance dire.

He bedded down as night fell, but just before the dawn
A sheriff's posse caught them and took them into town.
The sheriff he just figured that he was one of them,
And threw him in the jail cell among the other men.

It took him some convincing to get him out of jail,
By then a strong infection helped him get his bail.
They took him to a doctor and just before he died
He told the doc this story and swore 'twas not a lie.

He related this whole story and then he drew a map.
X marks Horse Head Crossing and X marks Castle Gap.
Years went by before the doc and his attorney traveled out
To dig for buried treasure. No Comanche left about.

The Indian wars subsided and on the frontier land
The Army did its job well and held the upper hand.
They could not find the landmarks though they left no stone unturned
And they could find no evidence of the wagon train they'd burned.

They say no one has found it, an entire treasury.
Perhaps the place where it lies buried no one will ever see.
For those that are still searching, I offer this advice
If one can ever view the map try folding it up twice.

Another theory have I about the hidden hoard,
Some markers are extinguished and have to be ignored.
The sandstorms of West Texas will quickly change the face
Of anything that's standing in that arid place.

Ten miles north of McCamey if you will drive or fly a plane
You look off to the right of the highway going toward Crane.
You will not need a compass, nor a highway map
You'll see as big as Texas the place named Castle Gap.

I've been there twice while hiking. The rancher gave permission
For me to make the journey on a Sunday morn excursion.
Some men have brought in dozers, and others a back hoe
To dig for buried treasure, but never found a peso.

This story's more than legend. This story's based on fact.
The Treasury was missing, when Benito's men came back.
The doctor and attorney in this story were quite sure
The man who told the story was dying with no cure.

BILLY SOL AND THE FERTILIZER TANKS

by Roy E. Peterson (March 30 2012)

A good ol' boy from Pecos, name of Billy Sol
Did something quite outrageous and hid it from the law.
A governmental program could pay the rent on tanks
Containing fertilizer so Billy said, "Why Thanks!"

Billy Sol was partnered with a man called LBJ,
Who in turn was VP under President JFK.
A key campaign contributor to the Democratic cause
Billy Sol was confident that he could skirt the laws.

Billy Sol claimed mortgages on tanks out in the field
Where anhydrous ammonia within the tanks were sealed.
He used the fraudulent mortgage scheme to obtain loans from banks
Using as collateral nonexistent fertilizer tanks.

He told one of his partners and said it with some mirth,
"I think the Ag inspectors, are stuck there in Fort Worth."
The good ol' boys got richer with profit from the deal.
The Democrats were paid off and none of them would squeal.

Billy Sol got greedy and planned another scheme.
Although it was illegal, it worked just like a dream.
He purchased large allotments of cotton based on land
That farmers would first purchase from Billy Sol's own hand.

Then he would lease the land back and allotments from the farm
He told the local farmers his scheme would do no harm.
After one year, was the first date to make payment, but who knew
That Billy Sol had told them to default when mortgages were due.

The plan went on unhindered; for several years it ran.
The cotton allotment transfers made him a wealthy man.
Though it was quite illegal these Billy Sol antics
He dismissed the allegations as just being politics.

One day his schemes collapsed. The judge said fraud's the reason.
Your cotton and your fertilizer are taking you to prison.
Out there in Pecos, Texas they call it Estes Sunday
When people hunt for fertilizer. Forget the Easter Bunny.

MY TEXAS HOMETOWN CONFESSIONS

by Roy E. Peterson (March 2012)

I claim a Texas hometown not where born, but raised.
I moved there as a teenager back in my halcyon days.
Coming from a Northern state I had a little shock
Because my new surroundings were made of caliche rock.

That was not the only thing to take me by surprise.
There were a lot of changes I had to realize.
In class I had to answer teacher with the phrase "Yes, ma'am".
And "lickings" made me eager to get with the program.

For those who are not Texan and don't know what I mean
A licking with a paddle made every school kid scream.
It helps you pay attention to what the teacher says
And never ask a neighbor if they would pass the "Pez".

If I had a quarter, I'd run to Mr. Mack's,
Where I would order Frito Pie and other Texas snacks.
A Moon Pie made of chocolate or pecan pie would do.
RC or Dr. Pepper to drink when I was through.

The eighth grade was my entry upon the Texas scene.
Puberty had hit me hard as I had turned thirteen.
The Southern drawl of Texan girls drove me up the wall.
I wanted to be with them, and loved them one and all.

A girl I fell in love with let me touch her inner thigh
The eighth grade desks were doubles and hid the things I'd try.
The music played was Elvis and Buddy's "Peggy Sue."
The girls wore crinoline hoop skirts, the meat was barbeque

My fantasies were heightened when I had my first real kiss.
I thought that I found heaven and dreamed in perfect bliss.
Parties there were monitored, but we played "Kiss, Go Walk, or Slap"
And sometimes in my homeroom a girl sat on my lap.

My high school days were special, now that I look back.
A Badger was the mascot, the colors orange and black.
Football was like religion. The town folk praised the team.
And if you were a player, you were held in high esteem.

A lot of things were happening at the Circus Drive In show
But they weren't on the big screen. They were happening down below.
Down by the Pecos River or Old Maid Springs we'd park
So we could spend the evening and kiss there after dark.

There were historic places where one could take a hike,
Or travel ten miles out of town if you could ride a bike.
Castle Gap was halfway on the road to Crane
And there was Horsehead Crossing that watered wagon trains.

Treasure hunters gather for a story that's oft retold
Of how a band of Indians stole Maximilian's gold.
And drove the laden wagons through the Crossing towards the Gap,
Where they in turn were set upon by marauders in a trap.

When one is hunting arrowheads and looking at the ground
Occasionally there's a glitter of a Spanish coin that's found.
Dinosaurs left their muddy tracks near the road that's headed west.
Where wildcatters find the oil and heavily invest.

Much closer and just east of town we have Humble Oil to thank
For building oil storage that's a million barrel tank.
A concrete bowl for playground for a folly that went bad
When the concrete it expanded and drained all the oil it had.

At night we were surrounded by fires on King Mountain
That burned the sour gases. It was something you could count on.
At times you'd smell the gases and thought that it was funny
To tell the one you're riding with "Well, dear, just smell the money."

The only trees that grew there in the searing desert heat
Were really scraggly bushes that I learned were called mesquite.
When I had just arrived there I saw something that amazes.
I watched from Badger stadium the rattlesnakey races.

My cousin, Joyce, would drive me if her father would allow
And ask me if I wanted a pink or purple cow.
At first I wasn't certain. What I expected was the worst.
But a cherry or a grape float would quench the summer thirst

I remember Pansy, the local character
Who lived still in McCamey and all the kids feared her.
She had been a beauty, an athlete to admire
Who was a star attraction as she walked on the high wire.

I'll write another story about her circus act
And how she fell from up there and nearly broke her back.
Sometimes she'd pull her wagon as she walked about
Sometimes 'twas overflowing with the junk that she'd checkout.

The girls were quite exciting from Joyce to Mary Lou,
Becky, Judy, Patsy, Donna, and LaDonna too.
Marilyn and May Carol, Mary, Billie Fay,
Beverly, Gayle, and Nancy I remember to this day.

Sharon, Paula, Barri, Barbara, and Bonnie Sue.
I stored them in my memory. What else was I to do?
My hometown was a garden of yellow Texas roses.
An oasis in the desert and fragrance for our noses.

You cannot put me on the spot to name my favorite.
There are still more I admired, Margaret, Trudy, and Jeanette.
I loved to watch the Badger Band with Majorettes so fine,
Especially when the times had changed and raised the skirt hemline.

Sometimes when summer break would come and it would start to swelter
I'd go across the alley and meet in a bomb shelter.
Sometimes I'd walk across the street and ten blocks to the pool
To talk with bathing beauties and hoped that I was cool.

I loved the Baptist churches and going on retreats.
And I enjoyed the music of the band that played, Night Beats.
I respected Sammy Long's advice and thought that he was super
At keeping order and the law as our local Texas Trooper.

McCamey had an airport with service from El Paso.
Trans-Texas Airways used to stop, or so the old folks say so.
Runway 10 was the main one with forty one hundred feet.
Runway 28 one fourth of that, twelve fifty to where they meet.

Some friends were going fishing and I clearly was invited.
My parents wouldn't let me go and I thought I was slighted.
I learned from them when they returned, but first I have to warn ya,
That they went fishing cross the border for strippers in Villa Acuna.

My mother taught the fourth grade, my dad cleaned the high school.
One thing that I remember, they preached the golden rule.
Though we weren't rich we had enough by common family measure.
The times I had, the things I did, are surely mine to treasure.

My memories of my hometown still echo in my mind
It was another era and everyone was kind.
A place where people spoke the truth and never told a lie.
I'm still a bloomin' Badger until the day I die.

MILLION BARREL OIL TANK

by Roy E. Peterson (April 4, 2012)

Two monumental errors were built from faulty plans
One next to McCamey and one at Monahans.
Two million barrel oil tanks were laid out in concrete,
But Shell forgot to calculate expansion and the heat.

The engineers had failed to check the underground substrata
They should have drilled to check the base and calculate the data.
Underneath the heavy structure they would have limestone found
That was not conducive to support the tanks on ground.

Shell had so much oil coming from their new found fields.
While every well they dug was shallow, they had tremendous yields.
The mammoth oil reservoirs were built for surplus oil,
But in their haste to store it they forget to test the soil

Oil trucks hauled in tanks full of crude by day and night.
Until they could build a pipeline, they thought it was alright.
Shell built a wooden roof to cover all the oil inside,
But could fill them only part way up no matter how they tried.

The concrete and the heavy oil crushed the limestone base
And then the trucks were used to load the oil back in their space.
The leaks were from the bottom and from the sides as well
Two million barrel follies that had been built by Shell.

They had to stop production, and try to cut the yield
Until a pipeline could be built to Houston from the field.
There was no good solution to repair the damage done.
So now the empty oil tanks sit staring at the sun.

They look just like a stadium built 80 years ago,
And kids still like to party there and sometimes shoot their ammo.
Someday I'd like to buy it and with a little toil
I'd bring an oil rig in and drill for all that oil.

PART IV

THE LIVING AND THE DEAD

Drawing by Edgar Allan Poe

SOMEONE WHO WASN'T THERE

by Roy E. Peterson (March 8, 2012)

My publisher told me face to face
Find somewhere with lots of space.
Concentrate, pick up the pace.
Somewhere hidden as your base.

The agent in the plunging blouse
Said to me, "I've just the house!"
Belonged to someone name of Kraus
Who left it when he lost his spouse.

"It's fully furnished, as you request
The owner only bought the best.
You'll be a very welcome guest
And get some quiet, get some rest."

I surveyed the mansion that very day
Wrote out the check so I could pay.
My description if I had to say,
"An Impressionist painting by Monet."

The mansion sat in velvet hills
With gardens framed by daffodils.
I rented it and paid the bills,
But not for finding silly thrills.

The agent said, "I hope you'll find
This home will give you peace of mind."
"Please don't think I am unkind,
I did not come here to unwind."

"I'm an author. I need to write
Sometimes by day, sometimes at night."
The agent smiled and said, "All right.
I hope the ghosts don't give you fright!"

I watched her as she walked away;
Her derriere full throttle sway.
Images in my mind a play
I waved and said, "I thank you, Kay"

The mansion came with cook and maid
Some nights they left, some nights they stayed.
The elder cook looked half sautéed.
The comely maid her breasts displayed.

One night the cook and maid were gone.
I had to stifle back a yawn
I heard the rain through curtains drawn
But then the lightning hit the lawn.

While I was sipping pekoe tea
The thunder almost deafened me.
I think the lightning hit a tree.
I jerked the curtains back to see

Cleft in two the giant elm
Half pointed to another realm.
The senses seemed to overwhelm.
Unbridled captain at the helm.

As I peered on, the slithering rain
Beat upon my window pane.
An image mirrored to my brain
Perhaps I'm going quite insane.

As lightning once again hit ground,
Immediately I turned around.
'Tis hard to write down what a found.
An apparition without sound.

I saw someone who wasn't there.
A silhouette upon a chair.
A maiden with a vacant stare.
I didn't speak. I didn't dare.

A flash of lightning from the storm
The ectoplasm had a form.
The shape I saw did not conform
To anything that was the norm.

The maiden sat there in the nude.
I think she was in pensive mood.
You may think I am being crude,
But beauty cannot be called lewd.

She rubbed her hand between her thigh
And then she turned and caught my eye.
First with a shudder, then a sigh
She turned her face up to the sky.

Then with another thunder clap
I heard a crackle, then a snap
While wispy clouds of mist enwrap
My mind as if I'm in a trap.

Although I like to write romance,
I dared not take another glance.
I didn't want to take the chance
Of falling in another trance.

As for the telling, I'll defer.
Of this postponement I am sure.
Someday I'll tell my publisher
About the night I spent with her.

POE WOULD APPROVE

by Roy E. Peterson (March 9, 2012)

Poe's nightmares inhabiteth the senses
In the past and present tenses.
Sepulchers of death in stone engraven
Crested by the maddening "Raven".

Shadows upon darkness and mystery
Chased with intriguing poetry.
Indulge me as I reminisce
And take you close to the abyss.

First with "Premature Burial" we may start
And follow with "The Tell Tale Heart."
Next the "The Fall of the House of Usher,"
Followed by the "Purloined Letter."

"The Mask of the Red Death" strikes a chord
Then read "The Murders in the Rue Morgue.
"The Pit and the Pendulum" and "The Black Cat"
"A Descent into the Maelstrom" and things like that.

"The Gold-Bug," "The Imp of the Perverse,"
"The Cask of Amontillado," it's getting worse.
"The Oval Portrait" hanging there
Should give everyone a scare.

"Eldorado" and Annabel Lee"
"The Bells" and The City in the Sea."
"The Raven" and the lost "Lenore"
Will never be heard from anymore.

IN THE DARK OF THE NIGHT

By Roy Peterson (June 2011)

In the dark of the night when the moon's out of sight
The phantoms are free to approach even me.
They are probably right to stay out of the light
And not let me see they have hostility.

Ghosts prey on the brain. They're seeking to drain
My good energy like the sap from a tree.
It is really inane that they're acting insane.
Whether he or a she, it's encompassing me.

I must concentrate, when the time's getting late
And avoid their advances when they're casting trances.
Inspiration is great, but I refuse to relate
To their play that entrances and their silly romances.

I can't let them see, they are getting to me.
I keep my own vow to not raise my eyebrow.
It's a quarter to three, and they must let me be.
The ghosts anyhow must be leaving by now.

MY SOUL TO TAKE

by Roy E. Peterson (April 4, 2012)

A mind more powerful than mine compels me to write
Between sundown and sunup till dawn's early light.
I am driven by a force or forces that penetrate my cranium
From my cerebral cortex flows prose from the "subterraneum."

My semiconscious state contributes to the somnambulistic Incantations
reverberating inwardly as though they're heuristic
Guiding, instructing, demanding. I cannot stem the tide.
Am I a prisoner, or am I the warden? Where can I hide?

Both must exist in the same superstructure. If I could name
The muse that invades my soul that I'm seeking to tame
And who opens the channels of thought, I would tell you.
Perhaps a spirit vector morphing which I have to subdue.

I channel perceptions, clouded instructions of an ethereal being
Unambiguous, yet indecipherable images that I am seeing
Floating in and out of my reality, or unreality, as the case may be
A fascinating paragon of the past and future that both haunt me.

A mind numbing psychic phenomena just happened to me.
With channels of thought open and receptors operating free.
I felt an acute preternatural sense an email message was amiss.
Titled, "60 Seconds with God." Subtext, "Let's see if Satan can
        stop this."

Besides the text and subtext, the thought to check my email
Was simultaneous almost with the transmission detail.
This was not the first time I experienced a transcendental
Whisper or image from that source and I'm being factual.

It was the first time she forwarded a message to me this way.
There wasn't anything I could send back to her or say.
The incongruity with the darker muse shattered my tranquility
And left my mind to wander and perambulate mentally.

The Yin, the Yang; the Good, the Bad; the white, the black
Now I had two clearly defined opposites that I had to track.
It was like a dash of cold water in which my conscious state
Like an antenna acquired signals, which I sometimes relate.

PHANTOM GIRL IN MY DREAMS

by Roy E. Peterson (March 2011)

I saw her again in my dreams last night as clear as I'm writing this
now.
The girl in my dream I know is right, but I really don't know how
To tell you the way she makes me feel, or where she could ever be.
I only can tell you I know she's real and that she was meant for me.

I have some clues that are in my mind and have to write them down.
I'm praying some day that I will find her in that Southern town.
She's not the model I had for her in my waking conscious state.
The vision was strong and not a blur, but my time is getting late.

I can start with the way she wore her hair: shoulder length and
straight.
Her skin translucent while sitting there. This is so hard to relate.
Her slender face framed by perfumed hair cascading from her head.
I really must try to get this right as I get up from my bed.

The love of my life has a modest laugh, not loud as some may be.
A quiet laugh, like a photograph as if sharing a secret with me.
She wore a white sweater I think was plain and had on tight blue
jeans.
The smile of a lifetime drove me insane as if in a movie scene.

We physically hugged and then we knew what we had missed so long.
Something inside that instantly grew and that we felt so strong.
We were both divorced with children grown. I told her I had four.
But all were gone now, none were home of that I'm very sure.

I kissed her on her lovely lips the taste much sweeter than wine.
Images like movie clips kept flipping through my mind.
I don't recall we even spoke, but a powerful love was there.
I felt the love when I awoke while playing with her hair.

Will she return again to me to tease me in a dream?
Or will she be reality, or in a movie scene?
Where will I find my phantom lady? The one I know is mine.
The one who's wearing denim and sweater cut so fine.

WHAT SWEET MADNESS

by Roy E. Peterson (March 2011)

What sweet madness overpowers my senses?
What great gladness from phantom caresses?
What joy and happiness my mind confesses?
You are the enchantress with magical essences.

When did I know that my heart was aglow?
When did it show that I wanted you so?
When did hello chisel on my tableau?
I felt the snow melt and lava to flow.

Where have you been? You're a perfect ten?
From whence come thou then? From the forest or glen?
Where yet again can I find your love den?
You're my perfect woman, and that's an amen.

Was it your perfume when you came in the room?
Was it your typhoon that sealed my doom?
Was it your dark plume of smoke in the gloom?
May I kiss your lips bloom ere I go to my tomb.

How did it transpire that I felt this hot fire?
How did I perspire as the flames leaped higher?
How did you inspire this intense desire?
You are the purveyor and I am the buyer.

Who shaped your hair on your face so fair?
Who can compare with such beauty so rare?
Who is aware of the things that you share?
You're my love affair, though its solitaire.

You're my Aphrodite in a diaphanous nighty.
You're my Venus brightly that burns so rightly.
You're my muse so mighty with body that's tightly.
Come to me nightly and make me feel lightly.

Did she come from the sea? Did she come just for me?
Is she my destiny for an eternity?
I am bound happily. I will never be free.
Through my madness I see, this was just meant to be.

Why do I dream? Are things just what they seem?
In the pale moonbeam there is so much steam?
Why does it gleam like a molten stream?
I want to scream from this ecstasy supreme.

THERE IS A SECRET GARDEN

By Roy E. Peterson (February 14, 2012)

There is a secret garden within my heart and soul
Where I have planted roses for all the love's I know.
The fragrance of my garden, when memory takes a stroll,
Pervades my inner senses, while visiting each row.

The yellow rose for Texas, the red ones for Virginia,
Entrancing blooming beauties await my admiration.
The white ones South Dakota, the pink for California.
A garden filled with roses all share my adulation.

If I could be a hummingbird, I'd flit among them all.
I'd sip their nectar carefully while hovering in space.
Then like a happy gardener I'd sit upon the wall
And drink in all the beauty as I surveyed the place.

My roses are preserved there. They never droop or fade.
Their perky petalled faces expecting my sweet kiss.
Whether in the sunlight, or whether in the shade,
My secret garden's beautiful, a scene of perfect bliss.

HEAVENLY BODY

By Roy E. Peterson © March, 2011

My muse is quite entrancing, one of the heavenly beauties.
I thank the Lord while standing, or at night upon my knees.
One of the nine sweet sisters born of Zeus and Mnemosyne
The brightest star in heaven and she was made for me.

Is it Clio the Muse of history? It depends upon my writing.
Or perhaps it's the fair Calliope, protector of heroic sightings.
I know sometimes it's Erato, the muse of love's poetry.
Their inspiration opens the mind and purges my memory.

My mind is incessantly active. I never have drawn a blank.
Apparently my three main muses are drawn to my memory bank.
I have never seen their faces, but sensed their powerful charm
As one would affect what's written, while another guided my arm.

PART V

RETROSPECT

Photo Credit: Kristin Kelli Crawford

I AM THE KEEPER OF MEMORIES

by Roy E. Peterson (February 11, 2012)

I am the Keeper of Memories in a scrapbook in my mind,
The senses there are quickened with snapshots I can find
Detailing in a second everyone I knew.
While flashing through the pages, I always think of you.

A rose within my garden can never smell as sweet
As memories I garnered and stored within my "Keep".
You are forever present and but a thought away.
I wish that I could tell you my memories some day.

The time will come I'm certain when memories left are few
Within the vaulted ceilings the etchings fade from view.
The time has come to write them so memories pass along
To all the ones who matter to make the paintings strong.

Out there beyond the sunset, when my days are done,
I still will keep your memory somewhere beyond the sun.
You may feel my presence in the breeze or by the trees
And then you may remember, I'm the Keeper of Memories.

ODE TO TOILET PAPER

by Roy Eugene Peterson (February 1, 2012)

When I was young and needed to wipe,
A Sears catalog page I would swipe
Across my bottom, but I would need
Several pages to complete the deed.

At the age of 13 we moved to town
And catalog pages would not go down
The porcelain fixture in the little room,
So toilet paper became the norm.

Modern kids will not understand
My love for toilet paper in my hand.
They really can't appreciate
That toilet paper can feel so great.

Oh, toilet paper how I love thee!
I use one sheet when I have to pee.
I think of you as a soft tree bough.
What would I do without you now?

I take several sheets and fold in two
To clean up the other thing I do.
And if I happen to cut myself,
I reach for you upon the shelf.

I don't care if you're pink or blue.
Just plain white will surely do.
I want to thank you for being there.
You're something all my friends can share.

IF I COULD GO BACK IN TIME

by Roy Eugene Peterson (September 16, 2011)

If I could go back in time again,
I wonder at things that might have been.
If I could exchange right now for then,
My world would change as I imagine.

I realize today just why and how
My life would be richer and fuller now.
And if the Lord would please allow,
A different lover, a stronger vow.

If I could go back to the fork in the road,
I would have carried a lighter load.
I would have been strong, I would have been bold.
But who then could say, who could have foretold?

I have been blessed. My life has been good.
I did all the things I thought I should.
But looking back where once I stood,
It could have been better, I know it could.

I'M YESTERDAYS FOOL

Song by Roy E. Peterson (February 7, 2012)

Chorus

I'm yesterday's fool for losing you.
It's all over now, I'll make it somehow
But what can I do.
I loved only you. And now we're through.
You did me wrong and now you're gone.

Verse 1

When I was in love sometime long ago
You were with me where ever I would go.
And I was sure our love would endure.
Our love was real for I could feel you in my soul.

Verse 2

What happened to us? What could it be
That caused us to set each other free?
And yet I have found that I was bound
I could not conceal the way that I feel for eternity.

Verse 3

My life filled with power, with riches, with things,
With golden pins, and jewels, and rings.
The things that I thought I never forgot.
It should have been you. I hadn't a clue what you would do.

A BIRTHDAY WISH TO A FRIEND

by Roy E. Peterson (February 19, 2012)

I wish you more than a special day!
I wish God to wipe any tears away.
His arms reach down to you anywhere
Enfolding you with my birthday prayer.

I wish you a joy filled rest of your life.
Free from pain and free from strife.
A time to rejoice in God's mercy and grace.
A time to savor at a gentle pace.

As gold is sifted from soil refined,
You are the essence of love defined.
We once shared a spark of love sincere,
And intimate nights while I held you near.

I'm supposing our love wasn't meant to be
As we drifted apart. Was it you or me?
Embers still smolder from a word or glance,
But they can't rekindle our past romance.

MY HEART WAS FOOLISH ONCE AGAIN

By Roy E. Peterson (April 2, 2012)

I woke today surprised to find
I had someone on my mind.
I knew her fifty years ago
Perhaps our friendship could regrow.

My heart was foolish once again.
I thought of things that might have been,
If I pursued a different course,
Or would I have the same remorse?

In trepidation I reached out.
I let her know without a doubt
That I was interested in her
And all the things that could infer.

Although another wanted me
It wasn't something meant to be.
I am selective, give me that
She loved her dog I loved my cat.

Since I am living all alone,
I wrote her, "Call me on the phone".
Although I had my reservation
Let's see what happens in conversation.

Perhaps because I'm growing older
That's why I am getting bolder.
In part it's overcoming fears
In part the urgency of years.

I'll tell you in another rhyme
What happened and in time
The key deciders of my fate,
While by the phone I have to wait.

PART VI

HOLIDAYS

A BRUSH FOR THE LEAD

A FURTIVE VALENTINE

by Roy E. Peterson (February 14, 2012)

I would have sent you roses.
I would have sent a card.
But how would you explain them?
I think it would be hard.

My message is what matters.
A Valentine's Day thought.
A secret kept between us.
More than I could have bought.

Furtive hugs and kisses
Have passed throughout the year
In messages like this one
And words that I revere.

Though miles are far between us
And years have passed away,
Another hug I send you.
On this red roses day.

IMPISH IRISH AND ST PATRICK'S DAY

by Roy E. Peterson (March 17, 2012)

From Donegal to old Killarney
Irish have the gift of Blarney.
Whether angel, whether rogue
I love to hear them speak their brogue.

I'd love to have a leprechaun
With pot o' gold stored on my lawn.
Rainbows always ending there.
For luck o' the Irish the gold he'd share

I wish my dog were an Irish Rover
And shamrocks grew like four leaf clover.
A Celtic lass with her red tresses
Flowing softly o'er her dresses.

I'd love to see the Emerald Isle
And Celtic women that beguile.
Then I'd like to eat and ravage
A dinner of corned beef and cabbage.

I'd like to learn what drove Oscar Wilde.
Was it the authors he profiled?
A well known author in his day
He wrote "The Picture of Dorian Gray."

Why did Bram Stoker write "Dracula"?
The police in Ireland carry a shillelagh?
Perhaps one evening down at the pub
I'd sing "Danny Boy" without a flub.

MEMORIAL DAY 1955

by Roy E. Peterson (April 6, 2012)

I recall Memorial Day in nineteen fifty five.
The little auditorium was filled with those alive
Who soldiered through a World War and then Korea, too,
Who loved their native country and flag, red, white, and blue.

I lived in the Dakotas in a town called Bonesteel.
Just before the program I heard the church bells peal.
The high school band was the parade there wasn't any more.
When they marched in to City Hall, the veterans closed the door.

A poppy cost a penny, a crimson paper flower
That wrapped around my button like everybody wore.
Mother sang the anthem and when the taps were played
My dad led all the veterans in a salute and prayed.

A roll call of the veterans, those who served and died,
Was read by an old Chaplain as family members cried.
Four coffins represented the different wars we fought.
The Civil and the World Wars, and Korea as they ought.

Then families got in their cars and went to visit graves
Adorned with cross and flowers and flags that blew in waves.
The veterans fired their rifles as the casings fell in grass.
Then kids like me got busy and picked up all the brass.

A glorious time to be a boy to watch the grand procession.
A happy time without a war and over the depression.
A time when patriots hearts still beat and passed it on to me.
Duty, honor, country. Liberty's not free.

Then we got together and met at grandpa's place.
Riley, Nola, Linda, and Karen and I said grace.
We had been playing hide and seek and had to wash our hands
In one of those old basins on one of those old stands.

While Uncles Ray and Dale with Dad and Grandpa hit
The croquet ball through wicker hoops with colored wooden
    mallet,
Aunts Cecil and Luella with Mom and Grandma too
Would fill the table full of food just like they used to do.

I wonder if in those small towns in places like Dakota,
Nebraska, Kansas, Iowa, and those in Minnesota,
Still honor vets who sacrificed their very life for all
The rest of us now living as their memories we recall.

IF THERE WERE NO CHRISTMAS

by Roy E. Peterson (December 2010)

If there were no Christmas, where would we be?
No tinsel, no light strings, no evergreen tree.
No one to show us the way we should go
With mercy for travelers who drive through the snow.

If there were no Christmas, when would we give gifts?
Who'd brave the blizzards? Who'd cut through the drifts?
Where'd be the carolers singing their songs
Of peace and goodwill and forgiveness for wrongs?

If there were no Christmas, then just tell me this –
Who'd hang the mistletoe, who'd give me a kiss?
Who'd play at Santa and deliver the toys
To good little girls and good little boys?

If there were no Christmas and Christ was not born,
We'd be little lost sheep all alone and forlorn.
We'd have no more model of humility
By one who was born so he'd die on a tree.

So keep Christ in Christmas, the least we can do
And keep giving presents for me and for you.
In memory of Christ the child who was brave
And came down to earth our souls to save.

I'LL NEVER FORGET
THE CHRISTMAS

by Roy Eugene Peterson (December 2010)

I'll never forget the Christmas we still talk about,
When stockings caught fire and made children shout.
When father climbed upon the roof to hang lights on the eaves
And fell off of the ladder in a pile of leaves.

I'll never forget the Christmas the needles got dry
They fell off the Christmas tree and made mother sigh.
Who spiked the punch and got everyone drunk
And crashed on the table, now who'd ever thunk.

I never saw such kissing beneath the mistletoe.
I never heard such smooching as we watched the show.
While aunts and uncles thought they were Santa Claus
We kids had all decided, to save our kitty, Paws.

I'll never forget the Christmas that set off a roar
When mom dropped the turkey and stuffing on the floor.
The cat was very happy to lick up all the grease
And then my aunt came crying as she burned up all the peas.

I'll never forget the Christmas the fireworks were stored
Behind the tree for New Years. 'Twas quite a hoard.
And as it neared evening, Dad plugged the socket in.
At first came a sizzle, and then a big din.

It must have been wire the cat chewed we learned
That started first sparking, then needles got burned.
Which set the box of fireworks ablaze in all their glory
I laugh when I relate this and tell you the story.

We quickly ducked for cover as a rocket hit the wall
The next struck the ceiling and plaster to fall.
Then to our amazement the Roman candles lit.
We crawled into the parlor, so we would not get hit.

I'll ne'er forget that Christmas as relatives went home.
They couldn't us leave fast enough and soon we were alone.
My parents started laughing what else could they do.
What a memorable Christmas! I began laughing too.

PART VII

UNLOCKED TREASURES

WISDOM FOR THE AGES

by Roy Peterson (February 20, 2012)

- If at first you don't succeed, try again. The damage you really can do could be massive!

- Words paint a picture colors only can dream.

- Don't walk in someone's shoes. Make a path for them to follow.

- Warm whiskey, white wine, and wild women are all incendiaries.

- There is always one more option of which you have not thought and that likely is the best option. (My Murphy's Law Corollary)

- I know I am not perfect, but I am self-satisfied.

- People who are wrong are the most easily offended.

- You are either for or against me. If you are for me, Heaven help you! If you are against me, Heaven help you!!!

- Military legend from an Efficiency Report: "This person failed to live up to the low standards he set for himself.

- If I wanted you to know, I would have put it on *Facebook*.

PETERSON FORMULA FOR SUCCESS

by LTC Roy E. Peterson (January 25, 2012)

Copyright ©

IT ADDS UP = SUCCESS:

1. Intelligence

There are at least seven (7) types of intelligence, so almost everyone qualifies. (See my book, "Magnetism to Marriage".)

2. Training

Training and education are required to develop abilities.

3. Ambition

This is a driver toward success, but ambition must be tempered by discipline and prayer. Blind ambition is really blindness to one's own imperfections.

4. Desire

Desire complements Ambition, but without Desire, Ambition is empty.

5. Discipline

A character trait that develops and sharpens mental, moral, physical, and spiritual behavior. Discipline brings focus on the tasks at hand and on those things that lead to success.

6. Support

You are not alone, nor will you succeed alone. Support from family, friends, the team, environment, religious leaders and institutions, educators, and trainers are all important in achieving success. Maximizing the support base and knowing that there are those to act as a safety net and to pick you up when you may first face disappointments give you the confidence to climb much higher. Never forget those who assist you, cheer you from the sidelines, and give their unfettered approval.

7. Upbringing

The preferred foundation for success, but poor upbringing can be overcome with the other elements of the formula.

8. Prayer

The quest for divine guidance brings calmess, confidence that one is pursuing the good and moral path to success, and completeness that is an internal validation and satisfaction with what one is doing.

DECISIONS, DECISIONS

by Roy E. Peterson (February 20, 2012)

Be the leader don't follow someone said.
And so the new "leader" came up dead.

Blaze your own trail, don't follow the route.
And so he got lost and stumbled about.

Follow your gut, don't follow directions.
And so the man made no connections.

Follow your wishes, don't follow the crowd.
They buried him alone in a funeral shroud.

Follow your dreams, not some advice.
And so he had to fix it twice.

Question the rules, don't follow them.
That's why man invented the word mayhem.

Do what you love, not what they say.
And so you will pay, and pay, and pay.

Be awesome, not safe, words that sound so good.
And so he was awesome while lost in the woods.

AVOIDING THE ABYSS

By Roy E. Peterson (March 10, 2012)

Everyone passes through life differently.
No one fits the predestined model exactly.
Free will intervenes in the process of perfection.
Environment often determines acceptance or rejection.

Strong will can overcome circumstance and element.
Everyone has potential for deviltry or living testament.
Evil intentioned are not redeemed by one act of kindness.
But one bad decision can result in cultural blindness.

One bad deed can destroy life, liberty, and relations.
We are the product of those around us and our associations.
Except for family, we choose those with whom we share.
Evaluate, caste off those who will drag us down. Select with
    care.

Avoiding the abyss is the essence of wellness and survival
Turning around is the only way of finding self revival.
Drugs, alcohol, and sexual diseases I can tell you surely
Are three paved paths to the inky mists of time prematurely.

Risky behavior including rides in vehicles that are speeding
May result in accidents in which one is at a minimum bleeding.
Controlling ourselves is the way to increase our fame.
Discipline and preserving reputation mean everything to our
    name.

EXPLAINING THE UNEXPLAINABLE

By Roy E. Peterson (March 10, 2012)

With trepidation I embark on a torturous quest
To explain some secrets I've kept close to my breast.
Even psychologists cannot clearly explain
The visions and passions that cavort in the brain.

Since I will never undergo the act of hypnosis,
I keep locked away almost every psychosis.
Relatives and friends may have strong fascinations
With delusions of grandeur or my hallucinations.

Now let me explain the unexplainable
How fictionalized accounts are thus attainable.
The contradiction between life lived and observed
And the telling of stories apparently unreserved.

Some secrets one must savor in one's hidden harbor
Safe from judgmental observers forever.
Better the treasure chests of stories n'er told
And keep the locks sealed to protect the gold.

Experiences authors must write unencumbered
Without full disclosure and keep them unnumbered.
Draped on the stories are fantasies imagined
Baring the soul without being burdened.

From the safety of the author's imagination
Words pour out in fictional transformation.
Restrictions that pervade the earthly existence
Are given free flight in ethereal brilliance.

FACEBOOK

by Roy Eugene Peterson (February 7, 2011)

Sometimes when I grow weary I sit and take a look
At all the friends that matter inhabiting Facebook.
I feel as though intruding, asking pardon for my stare
As I sip my coffee slowly, sitting in my chair.

Is it alright to answer some question that they raise?
What are they really looking for? Some help? A little praise?
Sometimes I wish they heard me. I wish there were a mic.
Perhaps just press the button, the one that says I "Like".

Should I write a comment upon their precious wall?
Maybe they don't want me to say anything at all.
I know that if I answer the whole wide world can see
The personal things I say there. What will they think of me?

How did an old acquaintance become a friendly face?
And want to learn about me, through questions on this space?
When did the world get closer impinging on my day?
When did I have to carefully prepare the words I say?

For all the world is watching to read just what I write.
Some friend will lol it, while others pick a fight.
But I just want to share some things that show just who I am.
A friendly Facebook denizen, perhaps a funny ham.

COFFEE SONG

by Roy E. Peterson (March 3, 2012)

Give me a goose of juice, Bruce. Give me a goose of juice.
Make me a mug of mud, Bud. Make me a mug of mud.
Pick me off the rug, Bud. So I can take a chug.
Show me a flow of Joe, Moe, Show me a flow of Joe.

Pass me a pot of latte, Dottie. Pass me a pot of latte.
I love a hottie latte, Dottie. I love a hottie latte.
When you give me a latte, Dottie, that's when I'm feeling naughty.
Pass me a pot of latte, Dottie. Pass me a pot of latte.

Pour me a handy grande, Blondie. Pour me a handy grande.
Make mine a local Mocha, Joka. Make mine a local Mocha.
Give me a loan "a" Kona, Mona. Give me a loan 'a' Kona.
Fill me a cup of Java Bobba, Fill me a cup of Java.

Throw me a slew of brew, Lou. Throw me a slew of brew.
Give some to my crew, Lou. Watch what they can do.
If you are cold and blue, Lou, coffee will get you through.
Throw me a slew of brew, Lou. Throw me a slew of brew.

I'M SORRY I'M NOT PERFECT

by Roy Peterson (March 30, 2012)

I truly am not perfect. I really don't know why.
Sometimes I use the bathroom. Sometimes I have to cry.
Sometimes I am forgetful. Sometimes I tell a lie.
I'm sorry I'm not perfect, but Lord knows how I try.

I have to ask forgiveness for half the things I do,
When I have slighted someone, or not worked something through.
When I have hurt some feelings, or made a friend feel blue.
I'm sorry I'm not perfect, but I will try anew.

I have to take a bath and have to wash my clothes.
I have to brush my teeth, as any human knows.
I have to watch the words I say and not be one of those.
I'm sorry I'm not perfect, but neither is a rose.

If I have made you angry, the devil's running free.
I'm not sure why I do it. Can we just let it be?
If I forget to help you, or drive you up a tree,
I'm sorry I'm not perfect. I guess it's cause I'm me.

I promise to be better, to watch the things I say.
I promise you true friendship and help you every day.
You know I'll always love you, but my feet are made of clay.
I'm sorry I'm not perfect. But Lord knows how I pray.

PART VIII

PETERSON LISTS

CHRISTMAS LIST FOR SANTA

by Roy E. Peterson (December 2011)

1. A Pear Tree without a Partridge.
2. Two baked turkeys.
3. Three French Maids.
4. The cookies you collect from homes.
5. Winning Mega bucks lottery ticket.
6. Twelve foot TV.
7. Thirteen foot door to get the TV in the house.
8. One year supply of Dr. Pepper.
9. Storage shed for the Dr. Pepper.
10. Cowboys and Chargers in the NFL playoffs.

TOP TEN SIGNS YOU MAY BE A SCROOGE, IF...

by Roy E. Peterson (December 2011)

1. The only spirits you see on Christmas Eve are in the free eggnog.
2. Your Christmas tree is a branch from a tree on the neighbor's lawn.
3. You "regift" all the presents you received.
4. Your Christmas tree star is a beer can.
5. You replace your burned out Christmas bulbs with ones from the neighborhood.
6. Your holiday decoration is a rotting Halloween pumpkin.
7. You water the sidewalk to make it icy for carolers.
8. Your Christmas meal is Rahmen noodles.
9. You eat the carrots from children's snowmen noses.
10. You think Ho, Ho, Ho is a chocolate cupcake.

MY LUMPS OF COAL FOR CHRISTMAS 2011

by Roy E. Peterson (December 2011)

1. Bank of America for trying to charge a $5 monthly fee for debit card use.
2. Christmas Horror Movies.
3. Federal Government for bailing out banks and not people.
4. President Obama, because of his actions in making the payroll tax impasse worse. First, he inserted a class-warfare tax on job creators. The President then demanded a permanent surtax on millionaires' income as the price for continuing a one-year reduction in Social Security taxes. This demand stalled the debate on both the payroll tax and appropriations bills. There is a good chance all Americans will have a lighter paycheck next year as a result of Obama's insistence on a class-warfare tax as a condition of a maintaining middle-class tax cut.
5. President Obama for finding a way to increase labor costs that must be paid on government construction projects, thus currying the favor of labor unions at a time when private sector wages decreased substantially. This means Obama and the Department of Labor have basically funded Obama's reelection with billions in taxpayer money hidden from the average taxpayer by buying the labor vote.
6. The entire Kardashian family, but especially Kim.

7. Stores who do not allow their staff to wish us a "Merry Christmas" for fear of upsetting some customers or the ACLU. I always make it a point to wish everyone within earshot a loud and enthusiastic "Merry Christmas."
8. Lindsay Lohan, Charlie Sheen, Larry King, and the entire Jackson family. They have also qualified themselves to be donkeys in a live Nativity scene.
9. Anyone who plays Farmville and sends me updates on their conquests.
10. People who are obsessed with being politically correct. Being politically correct is not in my DNA, because I come from Texas!

TEN THINGS I LEARNED NOT TO GIVE A WOMAN AS A CHRISTMAS GIFT

by Roy E. Peterson (December 2011)

1. Gift Certificate for Weight Watchers.
2. Sharp objects that could be used against you.
3. Anything from an infomercial.
4. Fake perfume or anything that says Eau de Toilette.
5. Anti-wrinkle cream.
6. Clothes of any kind. You don't really know her taste and she will quiz you as to why that item was bought for a long time.
7. Flannel lingerie. That is an insult from which you may never recover.
8. Fruit cake. Women think a gift is how you think of them.
9. A disguised gift for yourself, such as a shop vac. You may not be found next year.
10. A plush toy that looks like a monkey. Review item 8 comment.

TEN MORE THINGS I LEARNED NOT TO GIVE A WOMAN AS A CHRISTMAS GIFT

by Roy E. Peterson (December 2011)

1. Gift Certificate to a Plastic Surgeon.
2. Fake diamonds. They do test them on glass you know. While on the jewelry gift angle, do not give any jewelry that is cheap and turns the skin green.
3. Hershey's Kisses instead of Ferrero Rocher or equivalent Chocolate.
4. Pepper spray.
5. Guns, especially if coupled with ammunition.
6. Monster truck rally tickets.
7. Cuckoo clocks or other annoying devices.
8. A cookbook. Just think of the message being sent.
9. A T-shirt of any kind with any message on it. It not only is cheesy, it can get you in a lot of trouble.
10. Never give a gift you gave her last year as well.

TEN GIFTS WOMEN SHOULD NOT GIVE A MAN

by Roy E. Peterson (December 2011)

1. Bath salts or scented candles.
2. Grooming products. Think of the message it sends.
3. Cheap necktie.
4. Opera or ballet tickets.
5. Chihuahua.
6. Box of frozen veggie burgers.
7. Embroidered hankies.
8. Pink sweater, or pink anything.
9. Celine Dion CD or any CD loved by a woman.
10. Any Movie on a DVD that makes a woman cry.

TEN THINGS I WANT TO KNOW

by Roy E. Peterson (December 2011)

1. Victoria's Secret.
2. Why are there no horses in horseradish?
3. Can mustard really be cut?
4. Why are Krispy Kremes soft and not crispy?
5. Who hid the Fountain of Youth and where can I find it?
6. Who decided the number one card (Ace) in a card deck was higher than the King?
7. You never see the headline, "Psychic wins Lottery"?
8. Why can't women put on mascara with their mouth closed?
9. Why is lemon juice made with artificial flavor and dishwashing detergent with real lemons?
10. What to do if an endangered animal eats endangered plants?

TOP TEN (FUN) NEW YEAR'S RESOLUTIONS FOR 2012

by Roy E. Peterson (January 1, 2012)

1. I will exercise less. My healthy friends have all died. They must have. Everyone else has aches and pains.
2. I will drive more slowly. I can't see the signs at the speed I like to drive anyway.
3. I will get revenge on all the people bad to me in previous years.
4. I will investigate going solar—at a nudist resort.
5. I will find out if Bridget Bardot is available for dating. I waited too long to ask Elizabeth Taylor!
6. I will stop asking young waitresses and secretaries for their phone number. I never did ask older ones.
7. I will stop using lol on messages so my friends will wonder how I really meant it.
8. I will find out why I never received the "Frauds and Scams" correspondence course for which I paid a lot of money.
9. I will not eat Mexican food and take a sleeping pill the same night.
10. Next time I will read the manual first before working on something.

LIST OF TEN THINGS I LEARNED IN THE MILITARY

by Roy E. Peterson (January 2012)

1. [From a Marine Colonel friend] "If you are explaining, you are losing."
2. [From another Marine Colonel at DIA] "Soviets can't create, only God creates." (I changed the report.)
3. The CIA is not the enemy, but their interests are not necessarily military interests.
4. If you are not first in line, you are already behind.
5. General's do not know everything. They depend on you for that.
6. Keep your weapons pointed down range. That is where the enemy is found.
7. The military way may not be the correct way, but it sure keeps you out of trouble with your superior officers.
8. The more work I did the more work I got.
9. Marines can't help it. They are trained that way.
10. Camouflage body paint is not a uniform.

LIST OF TEN THINGS I LEARNED IN THE ARMY

by Roy E. Peterson (January 2012)

1. Command decisions are not ratified by a 2/3rds majority.
2. Military vehicles are not used to flatten things.
3. Not to explain Army actions to incredibly moronic members of the press.
4. Army Mules are sacred. Navy Goats make good barbeque.
5. Congress cannot keep military secrets, so don't tell them.
6. Corollary to #5: Congress cannot handle the truth.
7. I can carry everything I really need in life in a backpack.
8. Courtesy really can be taught.
9. Life is short for the stupid and much shorter if they are in the Army.
10. Bad weather and holidays are a good time to attack the enemy.

WHY I AM NOT A MUSLIM

Not that the thought ever crossed my mind

by Roy E. (January 2012)

1. I like to eat pork, especially ham, sausage, and barbeque ribs.
2. I like to see what women really look like.
3. I like Freedom and Democracy, not a Theocracy.
4. I do not approve of domestic violence (The Koran says for men to hit their wives if they disobey).
5. I am too old to kneel on a prayer rug five times a day.
6. I would never join the Antichrist.
7. I like to take baths.
8. Christian names are easier to spell.
9. Mohammed wrote that at night "the sun sets in a muddy spring." This was a Muslim belief for centuries.
10. Mohammed's cure for ailments was to drink camel urine. I do not own a camel.
11. I am not a bigamist and do not believe in slave girls for sex.
12. I am not a pedophile (Mohammed wanted 12 year old girls).

MY TEN FAVORITE
POLITICAL QUOTES

by Roy E. Peterson (February 2012)

1. The power to tax is the power to destroy.
    (US Chief Justice John Marshall)

2. No man's property is safe when Congress is in session.
    (Will Rogers)

3. The only way for evil to triumph is for good men to do nothing.
    (Edmund Burke)

4. That government is best which governs least.
    (Henry David Thoreau)

5. Democracy is the worst form of government, except for all others.
    (Winston Churchill)

6. Ask not what your government can do for you.
    Ask what you can do for your government.
    (President John F. Kennedy)

7. Politics is the art of looking for trouble, finding it whether it exists or not, diagnosing it incorrectly, and applying the wrong remedy.
    (Ernest Benn)

8. Politics is the gentle art of getting votes from the poor and campaign funds from the rich, by promising to protect each from the other.
    (Oscar Ameringer)

9. Under democracy one party always devotes its chief energies
    to trying to prove that the other party is unfit to rule - and
    both commonly succeed, and are right.
    (H.L. Mencken)

10. Speak softly and carry a big stick.
    (President Theodore Roosevelt)

TEN TEXAS CULTURAL EXPRESSIONS I LEARNED WHEN I MOVED TO TEXAS

by Roy E. Peterson (February 2012)

1. I don't care if it hairlips the bear.
2. I don't cotton to that.
3. Friendly as fire ants.
4. He'd foul up a two car funeral.
5. Scarce as horny toad fangs.
6. He's got a burr under his saddle.
7. He can eat corn through a picket fence.
8. Bigger'n Dallas.
9. Like a Blue Norther'.
10. Get your cotton pickin' hands off my stuff.

TEN MORE TEXAS CULTURAL EXPRESSIONS

by Roy E. Peterson (February 2012)

1. Like ugly on an ape.
2. If her brains were dynamite she couldn't blow her nose.
3. He could draw a pat hand from a stacked deck (lucky).
4. Hot as a two dollar pistol.
5. Built like a brick outhouse.
6. He'd worry the warts off a frog.
7. He can talk the legs off a table.
8. Better than an RC Cola and a moonpie.
9. Dumb as dirt.
10. Slicker than fried lard.

MY LAST TEN LIST OF TEXAS CULTURAL EXPRESSIONS

by Roy E. Peterson (February 2012)

1. That dog don't hunt.
2. Uglier'n sin.
3. Old as the hills.
4. Like a cat on a hot tin roof.
5. He's not worth the dynamite to blow him up.
6. She can talk a blue streak.
7. She was madder'n all git out.
8. I'm so sick I'd have to get better to die.
9. He's as crooked as a dog's hind leg.
10. She's so ugly she has to sneak up on a glass of water.

"WHAT ARE YOU DOING AT THE SUPERMARKET TODAY?"

[Inspired by a friend who was asked the question and wanted a good rejoinder]

by Roy E. Peterson (February 19, 2012)

1. I shop for food once a year and bury a year's supply in my backyard.
2. I am looking for my car that I lost in the last storm.
3. My entertainment is playing with the automatic electric doors.
4. Today I plan on sampling all the air fresheners.
5. They ran out of condoms at the drug store.
6. Come join me and we'll TP the fruits and vegetables.
7. I came for the shopping cart races. Have you entered?
8. I'm, going to play "Marco...Polo" with my grandchildren.
9. I'm casing the joint.
10. I'm going to buy enough Jello for the wrestling contest.

JOURNEYS AND TRIPS

by Roy E. Peterson (March 2, 2012)

1. Make sure the first step is in the right direction.
2. The first step on a journey is worth a thousand words.
3. If your destination isn't heaven, I can help you go to hell.
4. Everyone goes on journeys. Completing them is the problem
5. Is it the journey or the destination? Sometimes both are important.
6. Columbus was less interested (though concerned) with the journey, but was focused on the destination.
7. Every journey taken improves with the telling.
8. Don't start a journey without a map (at least in your mind) and a destination in mind.
9. One must prepare properly for whatever journey one intends. If it may snow, prepare for a blizzard.
10. Going on a journey should be like the Military Intelligence Preparation of the battlefield. The preparation factors are Weather, Environment, and Terrain (W.E.T.).

HOROSCOPES FOR MARCH 4-10

By Roy E. Peterson (March 3, 2012)

1. Aquarius: You just had a birthday. If you want to see your next one grow up.
2. Pisces: Don't eat fish. You may destroy your sign.
3. Aries: Butting off is better than butting in.
4. Taurus: Keep your bull to a minimum.
5. Gemini: Buy two of everything.
6. Cancer: This is a good week to wear a disguise.
7. Leo: Roar a lot, but do it at home.
8. Virgo: You are the reason for the X factor.
9. Libra: Take off the blindfold and weigh everything carefully.
10. Scorpio: Everyone should be afraid of you this week.
11. Sagitarius: Make confident decisions with gusto. They will be wrong of course.
12. Capricorn: You are susceptible to snow jobs by incompetents.

CONSEQUENCES OF FOLLOWING ADVICE

by Roy E. Peterson (March 3, 2012)

1. "Let a smile be your umbrella."
-----You will catch cold in the rain.

2. "To err is human. To forgive is Divine."
-----Actually to forgive is asking for it to happen again.

3. "When in Rome do as the Romans do."
-----But forget the orgies.

4. "Fight fire with fire."
-----Both men's houses are turned to ashes.

5. "Waste not, want not."
-----You can become the greatest hoarder of all time.

6. "Live like there is no tomorrow."
-----And there likely won't be.

7. "What goes around comes around."
-----Especially boomerangs.

8. "A bird in the hand is worth two in the bush."
-----Unless the one in hand is a mad hawk and the two in the bush are fat turkeys.

9. "It is better to give than to receive."
-----Especially if we are talking about advice, punishment, or old clothes.

10. "Be yourself."
------This may be the worst advice of all time.

ADVICE FOR A GOOD DAY

By Roy E. Peterson (March 3, 2012)

1. Astonish someone. Do the right thing.
2. Consider the advisor before applying the advice.
3. If our advice is so good, we should have done it ourselves.
4. Where there is a will, there is a way. Especially if the will comes from a rich uncle.
5. Anyone can give advice. Few can take it.
6. A person without advice is a person without thoughts.
7. To do nothing is often the best course of action.
8. Wise men do not dispense with advice unless asked.
9. Fools often fail to take their own advice, but everyone wishes they had.
10. I advise everyone not to die unless they are prepared to deal with the results.

MY FAVORITE QUOTES

Collected by Roy E. Peterson (March 2012)

1. "Two things are infinite: the universe and human stupidity; and I'm not sure about the universe."
— Albert Einstein

2. "Be yourself; everyone else is already taken."
— Oscar Wilde

3. "You only live once, but if you do it right, once is enough."
— Mae West

4. "If you tell the truth, you don't have to remember anything."
— Mark Twain

5. "It is better to remain silent and be thought a fool than to open one's mouth and remove all doubt."
— Abraham Lincoln

6. "Always forgive your enemies; nothing annoys them so much."
— Oscar Wilde

7. "A friend is someone who knows all about you and still loves you."
— Elbert Hubbard

8. "Life is what happens to you while you're busy making other plans."
— John Lennon

9. "That which does not kill us makes us stronger."
— Friedrich Nietzsche

10. "I have not failed. I've just found 10,000 ways that won't work."
— Thomas A. Edison

LENT BENT

What I Would Give Up If I Paid Attention to Lent

by Roy E. Peterson (March 6, 2012)

1. Duct taping people to chairs.
2. Putting wet superglue on keyboards.
3. New Year's Resolutions.
4. Ironing my underwear.
5. Using my hand as a tissue.
6. Telling bad jokes.
7. Eating my own cooking.
8. Stopping at green lights.
9. Soy products.
10. Looking for the Fountain of Youth.

TEN WAYS YOU KNOW IT'LL BE ONE OF THOSE DAYS

by Roy E. Peterson (March 3, 2012)

1. The predicted high for the day is at 3AM.
2. You can't find the cat and the dog is looking guilty.
3. You can't find your car keys and then you can't find your car.
4. You hear sirens and they all seem to stop in front of your house.
5. The water stops while you are taking a shower.
6. You wake up and the house is filled with smoke.
7. You place ten phone calls and no one answers.
8. Your horoscope says, "Forget it. Stay in Bed."
9. The trash can fell over and your junk is all over the neighborhood.
10. You are stopped at a checkpoint and can't find your license, registration, or proof of insurance.

See! You are having a better day than these people already.

PART IX

INTROSPECTION

BAGGAGE

by Roy Eugene Peterson (December 2011)

Baggage is the guilt we bear
Things that we can never share.
Weights upon our inner core.
Burdens that we keep in store.

Baggage is something we control.
We need to purify the soul.
Get rid of it is my advice.
You have the power to excise.

Get rid of baggage in your lives.
I'm not including former wives.
They are still a part of me
Though they think they set me free.

I thought that we would never part.
I'm romantic in my heart.
Seems they saw it otherwise,
Since they married other guys.

ROSES AND DIRT BAGS

by Roy E. Peterson (March 2012)

I have a rating system for those I love and for those I despise.
A very simple method for delineating values with one through five.
Five roses is reserved for those most valued in my life.
Five dirt bags for those against whom I will strive.

IF I WERE AN ANIMAL, WHICH ONE WOULD I BE?

by Roy E. Peterson (April 4, 2012)

If I were an animal, where would I be?
Down on the ground or up in a tree?
Perhaps in the sky flying in a vee?
Or swimming around down under the sea?

If I were an animal, how would I hide?
Perhaps in a burrow where I could abide.
A good camouflage I sure would have tried.
Or hidden myself down under the tide.

If I were an animal, what could I do
So I could avoid the fate of a zoo?
Run faster than wind, fly high in the air?
Use razor sharp claws, or have teeth that can tear?

If I were an animal, who would I be?
A soft Teddy Bear , soft, snuggly.
A mistress to carry me under her arm
To hug me a lot and keep me from harm.

THE POET AND THE PAINTER: INTROSPECTION

by Roy E. Peterson (April 5, 2102)

I fully understand now how all the poets feel.
They don't know if there's anyone who thinks their thoughts are real.
A poet to be worth the read must open up their soul
And thoughts for crass inspection; amusement sometimes cruel.

I remember reading once, "People will talk you know."
They'll comment on the fantasies; dark places that you go
To shed some light of wisdom, or open up the mind.
The common folk will twitter, but they're the ones who're blind.

A poet is a painter, who uses words for color;
An artist of a special sort, a penitent at the altar;
Observant and romantic; creative; fervent master
Of more than rhyme and reason, a pedant and a crafter.

The paper is the canvas, the desk top is the easel.
The pen in place of paintbrush, the palette is the sepal.
The words evoke the image, as color strikes the senses;
The poet like the artist, in past and present tenses.

Some poets write of shadows. Some poets write of beauty.
Some poets write of history. Some poets write of duty.
Some poets write love sonnets. Some poets, allegory.
Some poets write the world they see. Some poets tell a story.

Beyond the world of senses, the poet paints the dream.
Alternative realities are more than what they seem.
Not everyone can hear them, or taste, or smell, or see,
Or reach out with their mind set; touch unreality.

Some people are afraid it seems, to look within themselves,
To buy a book of poetry to place on dusty shelves.
Although I know some do this, buy Edgar Allan Poe.
A false pretense of intellect is often just for show.

Please let me share a secret. All poets have a need
To feel their work's appreciated like starving artists feed
Upon some kind approval, some passing accolade.
To counter all the ridicule of which they are afraid.

ON GREATNESS

by Roy E. Peterson (April 15, 2012)

It's often hard to recognize
The greatness one exemplifies.
The greatness of a person lies
Within the heart; behind the eyes.

The platinum parent, the friend of gold
It matters not if young or old.
Their greatness may remain untold
Yet somehow they still fit the mold.

A Christian is required first
The Living Water slakes their thirst.
In God's love they are immersed
And real happiness they disbursed.

The greatest have a moral code
They always take the narrow road.
Their inner strength doth not erode.
They always share another's load.

They may be someone near at hand.
A person who will take a stand.
Someone the world may think is bland.
A member of the angel band.

Beauty will fade and muscles too.
Greatness comes from things they do.
Wisdom is another good clue
And patience to see all things through.

The greatest aren't afraid to say
Please watch your step, tread well today.
Take time for God, his word obey,
Or for your sins you'll have to pay.

Look close around you. Cogitate!
Think of someone you believe's great.
Try to follow and emulate.
Study their actions; how they operate.

Love is the binder. It is the glue.
The keystone trait found in so few.
The greatest ones I ever knew
Never said things they thought untrue.

Fame is fleeting and like the sun
It fades from view when day is done.
Great in God's scheme has just begun,
When the course of life they've run.

SOME THINGS DRIVE ME CRAZY

by Roy E. Peterson (April 18, 2012)

Some things drive me crazy, some things cuckoo.
Some drive me wild and then there is you!
At you first you will write in a friendly way,
But then I can't believe what you have to say.

Got up in the morning to do some work.
Read your new email calling me a jerk.
Then I get a message, "Oh, never mind."
According to the latest you are being kind.

Reading your letters, tell you what I found
Much like a pinball I get bounced around.
I'm like the net for your circus act.
I always try to catch you and have learned to react.

Maybe it's the hormones that induce the mood.
Maybe it's the water or some foreign food.
Maybe it's the weather or a strained relation.
Maybe it's the figment of imagination.

"How do I love thee, let me count the ways,"
Like an E. Barrett Browning in a purple haze.
I listen on the phone and read every word
And try not to let on when you are absurd.

Perhaps I should tell you it is only fair
If you're going crazy, I am almost there.
Together we'll laugh and have some fun
Like two crazy people in the noonday sun.